WITHDRAWN
FROM
COLLECTION

ASIA

E

H

FRICA

O

J

P

I

INDIAN OCEAN

A

AUSTRALIA

F

Z

M

To Milo and Khalil
for inspiring me always
and to Kenneth.

• Claudia •

For Isabel and James,
little citizens
of this big world.

• Nan •

TRIBAL ALPHABET

ILLUSTRATIONS BY
CLAUDIA PEARSON

TEXT BY
NAN RICHARDSON

AN UMBRAGE EDITIONS BOOK

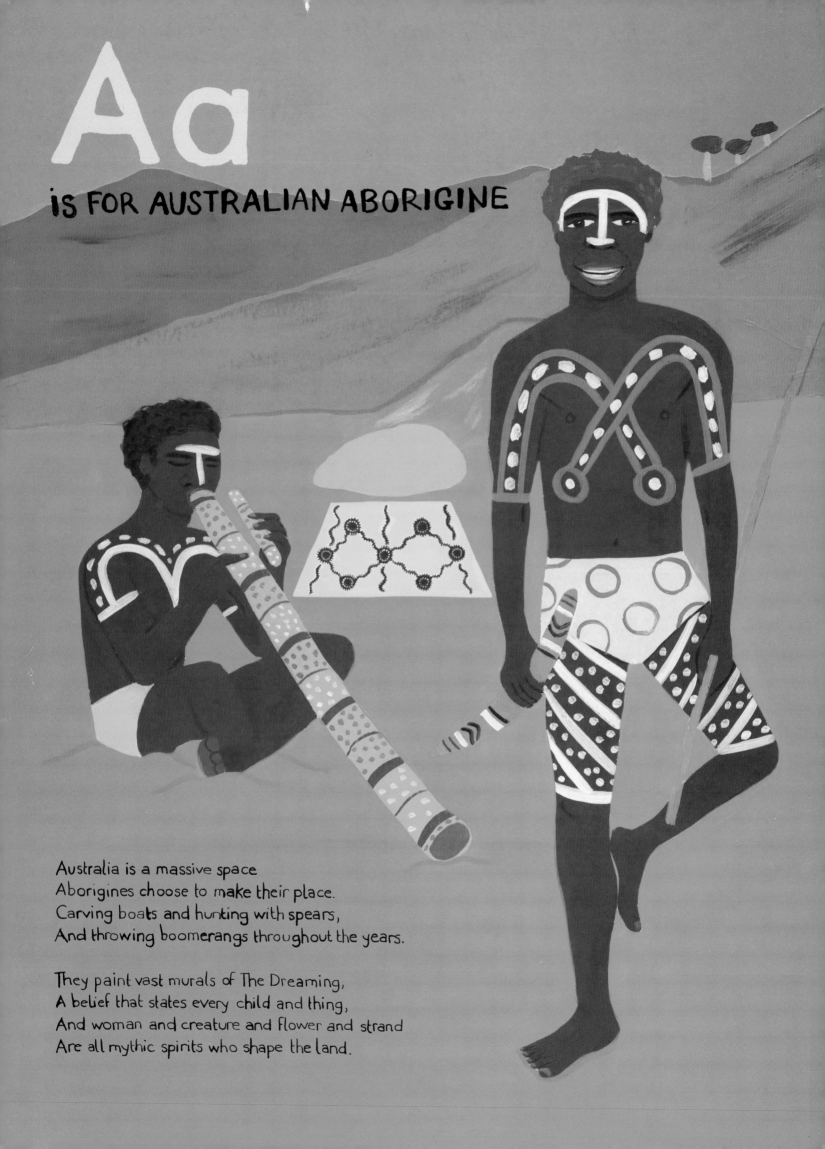

Aa
IS FOR AUSTRALIAN ABORIGINE

Australia is a massive space
Aborigines choose to make their place.
Carving boats and hunting with spears,
And throwing boomerangs throughout the years.

They paint vast murals of The Dreaming,
A belief that states every child and thing,
And woman and creature and flower and strand
Are all mythic spirits who shape the land.

B b
IS FOR BASQUE

Basques live in the mountains of France and Spain
Speaking a language that's not the same.
The games they play and the drinks they drink
Make their culture quite unique.

Their origins are a mystery
And have been lost to history
But the Basques take pride in their mysterious past,
And Euskadi culture remains steadfast.

Cc

IS FOR CHEROKEE

The Cherokee nation of seven clans
Once lived across North American lands,
But colonization forced them along
The Trail of Tears–yet they stayed strong.

Struggling now to maintain tradition
Finding meaning in nature a sacred mission
They stomp dance to Unetlanv (who created earth and sky)
And play a marble game: di-ga-da-yo-s-di.

Dd

IS FOR DOGON

The Dogon of Mali believe the world began
With one egg filled with two, a woman and a man.
The egg hatched too early, man and woman split apart
That's why the world has had two genders from the start.

While the Dogon once lived in cave villages on cliffs,
Now they have thatched homes (not quite as stiff).
But if their three tribes (Awa, Binu, Lebe) have, over time, changed
With dances, costumes, and masks, their culture remains.

E e
is FOR EVENK

Traveling across Siberian streams by canoe
The Evenk have land from Manchuria to the Arctic Ocean blue
In the north are the herders, raising reindeer and all
In the south are the farmers down by Lake Baykal.

But their land has been plundered for minerals and oil
Causing the death of bear and elk, the erosion of soil.
Now the ancient saying "No reindeer, no Evenk"
Is perilously close to true.
How will disaster for these nomads
Not ensue?

Ff
IS FOR FIJIAN

On the 800 islands that make up Fiji's nation
Live peoples speaking Hindustani, English, and Fijian.
Fijians sail from island to island on the ocean blue
Their homes they call bures, their clothing sulu.

They greet visitors with kava, to refuse this drink is rude.
Ginger, yams, and rice are some Fijian food.
They're close with their families, but strangers they shun
(A Fijian's village is not for exhibition).

Gg

IS FOR GARIFUNA

When an oppressive slave ship crashed fateful
Some Nigerian slaves escaped serendipitously.
These Nigerian orphans were taken in by Cari
And became Garifuna from swampy Belize.

Traditionally women care for the crops
Of rice, beans, corn, and manioc.
The men sing laremuna wadauman
While fishing all day and rowing along.

Hh

is FOR HMONG

Hmong come from mountains of Thailand and Laos
But wars caused the people to scatter in chaos
To China and Thailand and the US of A.
They are finding their culture again today.

They tell their stories on quilts that they craft
Stories of multiple souls and life's predestined path,
Excellent farmers, growing rice, poppies, and maize
Though still not free from persecution,
The Hmong won't change their ways.

Ii

IS FOR IFUGAO

In the mountainous interior of northern Luzon
Live the Ifugao people whose culture lives on.
They believe that each place, each person, or thing
Has a spirit inside it and is a being.

Yearly they race on their scooters of wood
Round and down past rice terraces and
fields full of fruit.
For sheer engineering and business know-how,
The Ifugao farmers deserve a big "WOW!"

Jj

IS FOR JARAWA

In endangered deep forests of the Andaman Isles
Live the Jarawan people who hunt by their wiles
By bow and by arrow, wild lizards and pigs,
Gathering fruits, varied nuts, and edible twigs,

In the Bay of Bengal with nets
and harpoons,
The Jarawa find shellfish by
sun And by moon.
We don't know their real
name as they chase
strangers away
Jarawa means "enemy",
And Jarawa they'll stay.

Kk
is for Kurds

A mountain people, without a nation
Kurds have struggled long for self-determination.
From Turkey to Syria, Iraq, and Iran
The tribes have wandered wherever they can.

Believing first in reincarnation and the magic number 7,
Seven good spirits; seven bad, fighting over the state of Man.
Now the Kurds no longer move around
Fighting for their rights and standing their ground.

Ll

IS FOR LACANDON MAYA

Into the jungle, never conquered
The last of the Lacandon still remember
The Mayan Golden Age in 50 BC
With writings, carving, and ceremony.

They migrate when the maize has exhausted the lands,
Hunting monkeys, birds, and fish with arrows in steady hands.
Each year to Yaxchilan they make a pilgrimage
Bringing copal as sacrifice to Chaac—their privilege.

M m

is for maori

Descendants of Polynesians
Who reached New Zealand by canoe
Their priests with magic powers
They called tohunga makutu.

They wear art on their bodies:
Tattoos of living and growing
And these complex curled designs
Tell a story well worth knowing.

Nn

is for Nukak

Along the Amazon Basin, the Nukak migrate
A tribe never contacted 'til 1988.
The Nukak hunt monkeys, frogs, and peccaries too
They fish for piranha in the rivers blue.

But now outsiders have sent in expeditions
And some Nukak suffer from disease and malnutrition.
Coca farmers and armies occupied their land
So the Nukak marched out, bow and arrow in hand.

Oo

IS FOR OROMO

Herding cattle in nomadic bands
The Oromo once roamed north and west from
Volcanic lands.
But these forest highlands, once utopia
Are now marked by strife in Ethiopia.

Both Muslim and Christian, they still believe in Waaqa,
The Creator who walked among men,
And safuu, balance in all life (very Zen).
Marriage is polygamous (one husband, many wives).
In the midst of much strife, their culture survives.

Pp

is FOR PENAN

There is no word for thank you
In the **Penan** language today
Sharing is taken for granted
Bornean hunters share their
smallest prey.

Now these nomads protect the forest
From the loggers who leave it bare.
The Penan won, the loggers left
Such victories are sadly rare.

Qq
is for Quechua

In the mountains of Peru, in houses of cold stone
Live an ancient people whose story's not well known,
Growing corn and taters, keeping herds of sheep
And llamas and alpacas, though their land is steep.

Their flutes and beaded costumes enact their oldest stories,
From times before Columbus, ancient, pagan glories.
They believe in forest spirits and shamans use a plant
With magic healing powers to understand and rant.

R r

is FOR ROMA

From India to Persia, from Istanbul to Paris,
The 4 tribes of the Roma have wandered long and long been harassed.
People of the highway, horse dealers from times old,
Blacksmiths, singers, dancers, their future is foretold.

They have a gift for magic, charms, palmistry, and curses shown
But they prefer to keep moving and shun a fixed home
They worship goddesses and believe in reincarnation,
And their beliefs, not boundaries, form the Roma nation.

S s

is FOR SAAMI

Earth and sea and northern arctic sky...
Though the Saami now live in cities
Their love of nature will not die.
Herders, hunters, and fishermen of old,

They used reindeer meat for food
And deerskins for clothing in the cold.
Out of Sapmi* now, the kata tents are gone
But in their new homes, the joik still plays a lively song.

Sapmi refers to all their ancestral lands,
part of Norway, Sweden, Finland, and Russia.

T t
is FOR TUAREG

Under the silent Sahara sky
The blue people are found nearby
Storytellers extraordinaire
They move their camps from here to there.

They live in dyed red tents of old
Women make camp, veiled men trade gold.
From ancient Phoenicia their alphabet derives
And their Imnaghgen (free men) tongue still thrives.

U u

IS FOR UZBEK

In the Central Asian heat
They have always farmed the land
Raising cotton, grapes, and silkworms
Weaving bags with their skilled hands.

Now turbaned men and trousered women
Go to chaikanas to drink tea
And have made tradition last
Through their famed embroidery.

V v

IS FOR VLACHS

City Vlach are merchants, country Vlach do roam.
With their sheep and goats, the villages they call home.
They share a common history, Vlach language, dance, and cuisine
Though they live in different nations, their identity can be seen.

Within Serbia, Bulgaria, and many other places
Of ancient Vlach history you can still find traces
But slowly their culture dwindles away
As assimilation takes its toll day by day.

Ww

IS FOR WOLOF

From the lush rainforests to the Sahara desert dry
The Wolof people are easy enough to spy
Because their sense of style is better than the rest
And women buy gay dresses to always look their best

Their faith is just as strong as their well-known fashion pride
The Wolof wear silver amulets with Koran passages inside.
Though many of the tribe have left and moved away,
The family, called the Mbokk, is still sacred today.

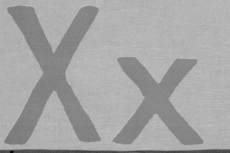

Xx

IS FOR XAVANTE

In the jungles and grasslands of remote southwest Brazil
The two clans of the Xavante live near rivers still.
The men wear wood sticks through the lobes of their two ears
To protect them from bad dreams throughout all their years.

The women weave strong baskets to carry their young
So their hands are always free to get other hard work done.
Though others' dams and cattle are damaging their lands
The Xavante live on to fight, giving the environment a hand.

Yy

is for Yupik

In Alaska and Siberia, where the weather's always cool
The Yupik respect the animals that in the cold sea rule.
Traveling in kayaks, or by sleds when all is ice
They live in igloos during winter, in wooden houses when it's nice.

Etching decorations, carving out of soapstone
For their tradition of leatherwork they are also well known.
They fish salmon and hunt seal, telling stories with loud singing,
And honor the souls of animals in ceremonies of thanks-giving.

Z z
IS FOR ZULU

Zulu nation! made up of many tribes
Today the people work in South African
Cities and mines.
But once that Zulu nation
Raised cattle and farmed grain
Believing in their ancestors
And in the power to make rain.

Every year they celebrate the harvest
With a feast.
They call it the Feast of First Fruits,
And everybody eats.
They sing and play the drums
To tell stories through their songs
They dance to symbolize
That the whole village gets along.

Glossary of Tribes

ABORIGINES (AB • UH • **RIJ'** • UH • NEEZ)

The Aborigines of Australia called that vast continent their home long before Europeans discovered it in 1788. Before then, Aborigines numbered about 300,000; their present population is about 130,000. Removed from their land, deprived of their traditional bush food, and devastated by disease, malnutrition, poverty, alcoholism, and violence, most Aboriginal people lived on town or were herded into reserves and missions. When through hard work they made these reserves into productive farms, that land too was seized. Many families engaged in land claim procedures, which are often difficult and expose them to new forms of exploitation. The Aborigines believe humans are a part of nature, intimately associated with other living things. These cultural beliefs and practices are known as The Dreaming, a story of the mythic spirits who shaped the land, bringing various species, including people, to life. The spirits left physical proof of their existence in the shape of certain landforms, which are considered sacred and central to Aboriginal religion, with men responsible for maintaining them and for conducting rituals around them. Stories of The Dreaming are recounted in Aboriginal paintings, which bridge the gap between traditional beliefs and contemporary Aboriginal life, as this artwork is now sold to tourists. Elaborate funeral customs and initiation rites renew their connection with The Dreaming, the continuing stream from which life came. Today in Australia, Aborigines have their own television programs, which help them to preserve their cultural traditions.

BASQUES (BAASK')

The Basques call themselves Euskaldunak and their homeland Euskadi. Originally Basques lived in their mountainous homeland in the westernmost part of the Pyrenees Mountains in Spain and France. Today there are about two million in Spain and 250,000 in France. Basque nationalists want to unite all their territory to form an independent state, something neither France nor Spain will tolerate. But they are proud of their specific culture within these larger countries and identify themselves primarily as Basques, even though modern Basques now live in major cities and are fully integrated into them. The origins of the Basques are a mystery—their language is unrelated to any known Indo-European language. Their distinctive folklore, folk theater, games, music, light-footed and acrobatic form of dancing, and a green or golden liquor called Izarra made from wild mountain flowers all define them as uniquely Basque. The national game, pelote, is played many different ways on a colorful game court using a series of baskets and paddles to hit the pelote, which means ball. Traditionally and politically an autonomous community, they tend to be skilled boat makers and fishermen.

CHEROKEE (CHER' • UH • KEE)

The Cherokee tribe was forced to move along the Trail of Tears during modern-day America's colonization. Currently, much of the tribe lives in Tahlequah, Oklahoma. Seven clans make up the Cherokee nation, each carrying on different and unique beliefs and traditions. Numbers play a large part in their belief system, with seven representing numerous things from purity to the directions—north, south, east, and west. The Upper world, Lower World, and Center are the additional three directions, the center being where humans are at any moment. Popular games include a version of marbles called di-ga-da-yo-s-di as well as stickball. The Stomp dance, a ceremonial dance performed after a long day of community socializing and feasting, is used to worship Unetlanv, the Creator, and is performed around a sacred fire, which burns all day.

DOGON (DOH' • GAHN)

Formerly known as Habe, a Fulbe word meaning stranger or pagan, the Dogon are a West African people living in Mali, believed by some to be descendants of the Ancient Egyptians. Within the Dogon are three sub-tribes: the Awa, Lebe, and Binu. While each sub-tribe has a unique spiritual focus, their complex religious beliefs are united by ancestor worship and respect for the land. Each village has a Lebe shrine composed of pieces of the earth to encourage growth. Among their rituals is the Awa dance ceremony, meant to lead souls to a final resting place. The Dogon possess a rich mythology with an interpretation of the universe in which all persons are both male and female. In the Dogon story of world creation, a cosmic egg containing male and female twins hatched too early. Because one of the twins broke out of the egg before the other, humans are forced to live with the imperfection of two genders. Migrations of this population towards big cities such as Bamako and, finally, the opening of the Dogon territory to tourism have together reinforced—irrevocably—the process of conversion to monotheistic religions, especially Islam. This evolution is detrimental to the reverence for ancestors and the clan traditions. Dogon artwork includes wooden masks of geometric patterns and figures that represent the first humans.

EVENK (EV' • ENK)

The Evenk are the indigenous people of northwest China and Mongolia. They are descendants of the Tungus, and the most numerous and widely scattered of the many nationalities of Siberia. The Evenk are split into two distinct groups: there are the reindeer herders, spread throughout Siberia, and the pastoralists situated in northern Mongolia and China. Traditionally, the Evenk were split into clans and traced their lineage paternally. Shamanism, a common traditional practice of many indigenous peoples, is in fact an Evenk word. The Russian Evenk have long fought for self-determination, while the Russians have attempted to change the nomadic lifestyle of the indigenous population and integrate them into Russian society. In 1930, the Evenk were organized into collective farms in an autonomous district now called the Evenk National Okrug. These Evenk are now mostly settled and have taken up agriculture as well as industry.

FIJI (FEE' • JEE)

Fiji is an independent nation in the South Pacific Ocean made up of more than 800 islands, but only 333 of them are inhabited. Native Fijians, who represent only 46% of the population, are mainly of Melanesian descent. Fijians sail from island to island in boats made of hollowed logs and live in thatched-roof houses called bures. The traditional sulu (the Fijian name for what the Indians call a sarong) is worn by both men and women—pants are rarely seen on either gender. The tribes tend to be very communal and family-based, with non-tribe members accepted into a village only if invited. A traditional alcohol called kava, made from the root of the kava plant, is offered as a welcome by most tribes, and to refuse the bland-tasting beverage is considered rude. The Fijians eat and farm sugarcane, coconuts, ginger, cassava, and sweet potatoes. Warfare among the various clans and tribes throughout the islands used to occur frequently, and it was considered necessary for a young man to kill an enemy before he received full status as a man. This custom is no longer practiced. Native Fijians own 86% of the landmass in Fiji. But under the Agricultural Land Tenure Agreement (ALTA) they get a negligible amount in return for the leasing of their native land—de facto discrimination against them… So native Fijians subsidize the economic development of the country as a whole and the wealth of the users of native land.

GARIFUNA (GHAR • I • FOO' • NAH)

The Garifuna descend from intermarriages between Nigerian slaves en route to the West Indies, who escaped during a shipwreck, and the local Caribs who adopted them into their tribe. They live in Belize, bordered by Mexico to the north, Guatemala to the south and west, and the Caribbean Sea to the east. The coast of Belize is lined with lagoons that several short and turbulent rivers flow through, while numerous reefs and cays (low islands) lay off its coast. Traditionally, Garifuna women care for crops and prepare food (primarily bitter manioc), while the men fish and sing laremuna wadauman (work songs). Their culture is rich, including their own dance, story-telling, and music called "Punta Rock," which emerged in the seventies as an expression of Garifuna pride, mixing traditional rhythms with electric guitar. While not associated with a single religion, Garifuna myths developed over time, eventually mixing with Catholicism, as well as Indian and African beliefs. Since World War II, small groups of Garifuna have relocated to Los Angeles, New Orleans, and New York City.

HMONG (MUNG')

Originally settled along the lower reaches of the Yellow River in China, many Hmong were recruited by the US during the Vietnam War in the 1960s and 1970s. With the end of the war, almost half a million Hmong had to flee from retribution by the North Vietnamese and the Lao government to isolated villages in the mountains of northern Thailand. Many of those that remain in Thailand live in refugee camps and await resettlement. In the past, the Hmong was made up of two groups known as the blue, who lived in the west, and the white, who lived in the east. The blue Hmong women were recognized by their beautiful pleated skirts, patterned with stripes, while the white Hmong women wore clothing similar to the men of the blue Hmong: baggy black pants, a wide blue cummerbund, and simple jackets with blue cuffs. The Hmong are also well known for their signature flower cloths with elaborate embroidery that serve as quilts and tell detailed stories about the Hmong's historical past. Today the Hmong live in United States throughout Minneapolis, Milwaukee, Texas, and Rhode Island, though many remain in China and Thailand.

IFUGAO (EE • FUH • GOW')

Ifugao (Tagalog for mountaineer) is a general name applied to the six groups of Filipinos living mainly in the mountainous interior of northern Luzon in the Philippines. The Igorot live in villages of raised, thatched houses and grow rice, sweet potatoes, vegetables, and fruits. Although no longer practiced, warfare (including occasional head-hunting) used to be frequent among some Igorot groups, especially those in the north. Most Igorot retain their traditional animistic religion, believing that every thing in the universe has a spirit, but today an increasing number are Christian. Because of their isolation in the mountains, the Igorot were less affected culturally and socially by the Spanish colonization. Unable to conquer the Igorot's territory (and the rich natural resources, including gold and silver, within it), the colonizers slandered the Igorot as primitive and savage. Unfortunately, this prejudice still exists in the Philippines, even though many Igorots have entered the modern world as professionals in almost every field. The Igorot take pride in their identity and today strive to change the stigma toward their mountain people and communities.

JARAWA (JAA • RAAH • WAH)

The Jarawa are one of the four tribes of approximately 35,000 pygmies living on India's Andaman and Nicobar Islands in the Bay of Bengal. The traditional way of life of most Jarawa is based on hunting and food gathering. The Andamese collect wild fruits, roots, nuts, rice, coconuts, and hunt wild pigs and lizards with a bow and arrow. In outrigger canoes they gather turtles, fish, and shellfish with nets and harpoons. The Jarawas live deep in the forest, which is in constant danger from industrial exploitation of timber, the island's main export. Jarawa is not the tribe's name for itself; it actually means "enemy" or "hostile people" in the Aka-Bea language. But because they have shunned contact for so long and there are no ethnographies of the tribes, it is not certain what their name for themselves is. Remarkably, the Jarawa survived the tsunami of 2005, even though their islands were among those most severely hit. Their ancient knowledge of the land alerted the tribe to the danger posed by the earthquake, and they fled further into the forest to safety.

KURDS (KURDZ')

"Kurd" is the ethnic name of thirty million people who inhabit Kurdistan, the mountainous border regions of southeast Turkey, northwest Iran, north Iraq, northeast Syria, and Soviet Azerbaijan. The tribes speak various dialects of Kurdish, and their religion and mythology varies from region to region. However, most of the tribes practiced some variant of Yazdânism until the Middle Ages, when many converted to Sunni Islam. Yazdânism involved a belief in reincarnation as well as in seven angelic beings that defend the world from their equal and opposite number. Yazdânists are still close to one-third of the population, and some Kurds still practice their own religion called Ezidism, believed to precede Islam. Kurdish culture is in fact among the oldest known to man, relating to Mesopotamian culture. Kurds still live in villages, cultivating wheat, barley, cotton, and fruit. They are noted throughout history for their struggle for self-determination and independence, which continues today, represented by their fight for a unified homeland that they would call "Greater Kurdistan."

LACANDON MAYA (MAI' • YAH)

The Lacandon are Mayan Indians living in the mountainous, heavily forested area of eastern Chiapas, Mexico. The Maya were the first people of the New World to keep historical records. Their written history begins in 50 BCE, when they began to inscribe texts on pots, bones, stone monuments, and palace walls. Today they number only about 500, and, until recently, stayed isolated from modern culture by living in tiny, widely scattered villages composed of several related families. The Lacandon move every few years, when the land they farm on becomes exhausted. As part of the traditional Lacandon religion, each village contains a temple in which copal (incense) is burned to honor the traditional gods. In the northern lowlands, Chaac the rain god is worshiped, and in times of need a chachnaac, or rainmaking ceremony, is performed. The Maya believed that when nobles died they became one with the gods, and that they dwelt in the night sky with them. From early times, the dead were buried under their houses, in which the family then continued to live. The Lacandon make a yearly pilgrimage to the Mayan ruins of Yaxchilan.

MAORI (MAO • REE)

The Maori descended from Polynesian canoe travelers who reached the islands of New Zealand in CE 900. Their oral tradition details their arrival from Hawaiki, a mythological homeland located in Polynesia on large canoes called waka; the canoes play a role in their genealogy, the equivalent of pilgrim ships in the US. Traditionally, the Maori live in villages (marae) of longhouses (wharenui) where Maori leaders are priests (tohunga makutu), believed to have special magical powers that can destroy humans, ward off attacks, and prevent natural calamities. Today, however, like many other tribes, the Maori people have almost all converted to Protestant, Catholic, and Mormon religions. Traditional art forms include poetry, storytelling, chants, dances (haka), and songs, as well as woodcarvings that decorate meetinghouses and canoes, though their most recognizable art forms are their distinctive tattoos. Generally etched on the face and buttocks, they consist of complex spiral designs, symbolic of growth, life, and movement, and often reflect group membership, rank, and status, expressing social and religious values. Like many other indigenous cultures displaced by others, they struggle with issues of poverty, inadequate education, greater risk of poor health, alchoholism, and depression which makes the preservation of language and culture even more important to the Maori.

NUKAK (NOO' • KAAK)

 The Nukak are one of six groups who together make up the Maku peoples, nomadic-hunters living near the Amazon Basin. While it is unclear where exactly the Nukak lived over the last few hundred years, we do know that it was in an Amazon jungle near San José in Colombia. Civil war, however, has affected the Nukak, whose land has been overtaken by drug lords and other poor Colombians who want to grow coca on Nukak land. In 2006, 120 of the estimated 500 remaining Nukak left their traditional territory, as the violence threatened to wipe out the tribe, and walked to the jungle community of San José del Guaviare. While the Nukak may have been forced from the jungle by the ongoing violence, they do not want to lose their history and traditions. The Nukak are supported now by government agencies and have been given land to live on as well as supplies for their journey back into the jungle, as some have decided to return. However, the Colombian government has been unable to guarantee the Nukaks' safety, and the tribe is threatened with extinction.

OROMO (OR • OOM' • O)

 The Oromo live primarily in Ethiopia, on land that varies from rugged highlands to dense forests. They have a long history of agricultural productivity thanks to the fertile volcanic soil. Formerly pagan, the Oromo believed in safuu, a cosmic balance between all things, animate and inanimate, as well as in Waaqa, which means The Creator/Heaven. In Oromo mythology, Waaqa used to wander the earth, among people. After an altercation he retreated into the sky, but was still considered to exist in all matter; Waaqa and Earth are inseparable. The Oromo today share three dominant religions, Islam, Christianity, and the traditional Oromo religion, often in fusion with one of the others. Marriage is polygamous, and each co-wife may have her own house. Traditionally cattle herders and warriors, the Oromo have migrated north and west, and while some still live in nomadic bands, today many are farmers living in villages or dispersed homesteads (if they haven't fled to other countries for political asylum, due to the unrest in Sudan).

PENAN (PEN' • AHN)

 The Penan are a nomadic people living in Sarawak and Brunei in Malaysia. In the 1980s, the Penans' land was invaded by loggers, threatening their settlements and their way of life, which is dependent on the forest. The Penan fought back, aided by the Swiss activist Bruno Manser. In 1999, the Penan were summoned by the Sarawak government after setting up blockades to stop the logging, though blockading has been illegal in Malaysia since the 1980s. The government, however, ruled in the Penan's favor, and the logging company was forced to leave and also to compensate the tribe. However, Bruno Manser mysteriously disappeared in 2000, and the Penan's way of life is still threatened. The Penan are continuing

to fend off the loggers. However, land already deforested has been turned into plantations and the Penan are losing the rights to their traditional land forever. While the Malaysian government formally recognizes the Penan's right to their ancestral land, in practice the loggers openly violate the protection laws.

QUECHUA (KECH' • OO • UH)

 The Quechua are a South American Indian people who, from earliest times, have occupied the central Andean highlands of Peru and Bolivia. Like other Incas, they speak the Quechuan language, play panpipe music, live in pre-Colombian-style stone houses, and practice a religion embodying pagan rites, rooted in the mythology of an obscure past. The Quechuans wear brightly beaded costumes to reenact some of their religious myths. Using traditional agricultural techniques, they grow crops of potatoes and maize in addition to keeping herds of llamas, alpacas, sheep, and pigs. There are highland Quechua and lowland Quechua (who live in the Amazon basin and practice a combination of hunting/gathering and agriculture). They believe in forest spirits and their shamans use the plant ayahuasco to communicate with the spirits and for cleansing/healing rituals called limpiadas.

ROMA (ROW' • MAH)

 The Roma are a tribe united by a common religion, but scattered across the world, as opposed to a single geographical location. Thought to have originated in northwest India and migrated to Persia and Constantinople (today's Istanbul), they are known for earning their living by singing, dancing, making magic, blacksmithing, and horse-dealing. The Roma consist of three main sub-tribes divided by language: Domari, Lomarvren, and Romani. Centuries ago, the Roma were among the last goddess worshipers in Europe, with beliefs in good luck charms, curses, reincarnation, and palmistry. Many of the women wear long skirts and practice drabardi, or fortune telling, while others known as rabarni or drabengi practice methods of natural healing. However, in the 1970s many Roma converted to Christianity, building Roma/Christian specific churches. American Roma have their own legal system. Legal matters are taken to the kris, a group of elders that hears and decides cases. Banishment from the Roma is the ultimate punishment.

SAAMI (SAA' • MEE)

 The Saami inhabit the Arctic and sub-Arctic regions of four countries called Sapmi, which include parts of Norway, Sweden, Finland, and Russia. Originally hunters, gatherers, fishers, and reindeer herders, a small portion of the population still herds reindeer. a traditional food. Reindeer herders don't let any of the reindeer go to waste, using the skin for clothing and shoes and the bones for tools and crafts. The seasonally migrating herder families were frequently seen in the traditional costumes of a colorful, decorated tunic and tasseled hats, and they lived in katas, tepee-like tents which pack up and make migrating easier. Most Saami now dress like other Europeans and live in permanent houses. They have been Christians since the 1600s, and before that practiced an animistic religion. Like most existing tribes, the Saami have embraced modern living, moving to cities outside of Sapmi and getting modern jobs. They still survive as an ethnic and cultural group, practicing traditional handicrafts and playing their traditional musical instrument, the joik, a source of interest and appreciation, locally and internationally. Like the Saami in Finland and Sweden, the Saami in Norway also have their own national Saami Parliament, elected by and from among the Saami. But Finland and Norway do not grant any special land rights to the Saami in their own Homeland, or to pursue their traditional livelihoods.

TUAREG (TWAH' • REG)

The Tuareg have lived in the Sahara Desert in Africa for centuries, controlling the valuable trans-Saharan caravan trade in camels, slaves, gold, and, until 1940, ivory. They are known as excellent craftsmen, making woven bracelets and other jewelry of ebony and silver. Calling themselves Imazighen, meaning free men, they are nomadic pastoralists living in traditionally dyed red tents made of animal skins. Tuareg are Muslim and are called the blue people because of the indigo headdresses that nobles of the community wear. The Tuareg men also wear a veil over their face that is seldom removed, even within camp. Roles of men and women within a family are strictly adhered to, with women making butter, collecting firewood and water, and making bedding and clothes from animal skin, while the men are responsible for selling in the caravan and for trading millet, sugar, and tea. Women have a relatively autonomous role in the Tuareg, a culture of matrilineal descent.

UZBEK (OOZ' • BEK)

The first inhabitants of Uzbekistan in Central Asia farmed the land, raising cotton, grapes, and melons along with Karakul sheep and silkworms. Known for their textile skills, women have embroidered handbags for over a century, with detailed images of animals on them, although all Uzbek people—men and women alike—are proficient with embroidery. To counter the intense heat of the region in which they live, the Uzbeks drink hot green tea. Dotting the mountains of Uzbekistan in every hamlet, are teahouses, called chaikanas. Uzbeks are very colorful dressers, with men wearing embroidered skullcaps or turbans of patterned material, and women wearing long trousers with knee-length dresses and floral headbands. Today, after years of being subjects of the Soviet empire, Uzbekistan is again a sovereign nation.

VLACHS (VLAK')

The Vlachs are descendants of the Thracians and Illyrians, the indigenous populations of the Balkans conquered by the Romans. Traditionally, the Vlach were farmers and lived in stone villages and hut hamlets in Walachia, a historic principality of Southeastern Europe, located in what is now southern Romania. It is a rich agricultural area, and grain production remains important to the Vlachs. Though traditionally mountain farmers and semi-nomadic shepherds, many assimilated Vlachs now work in the cities, predominantly as merchants. Today the term "Vlach" is a blanket moniker for the modern day Latin peoples of Central and Eastern Europe who speak Eastern Romance languages. (Vlach has also been used as a pejorative name for shepherds and farmers on the outskirts of the Eastern European nations, particularly outside of Romania.) Most Vlachs now consider themselves Hungarian, Serbian, Moldovian, and Romanian.

WOLOF (WOO' • LAF)

The Wolof people live predominantly in Senegal, from the lush rainforests to the dry Sahara desert. Of Muslim faith, their sense of style distinguishes the Wolof. Known as the trendsetters of West Africa, they believe what you wear says a lot about you. Often women end up in debt just to be sure they maintain appearances, wearing elaborate dresses, hairstyles, and makeup. Their most popular jewelry, an amulet, often contains a small paper with beautifully written sections from the Koran, combining faith and fashion into one piece of art. Traditionally practitioners of polygamy, family units often lived together, with wives, children, and brothers all on a single compound in small villages. This traditional extended familial and social network is called a Mbokk. Today, however, the Wolof have moved to cities where they get jobs as merchants and traders or live in rural areas, often as peanut farmers. Many Wolofs have also immigrated to New York City.

XAVANTE (SHA • VAN' • TE)

The Xavante live in houses built by the women in a horseshoe pattern, usually facing a river, in both the jungles and the grasslands of Eastern Mato Grosso in Brazil. Two clans make up the Xavante, the âwaw and the po'reza'õno. Marriages are only allowed between members of the opposite clan, and polygamy is often practiced. Famous for their log races, the clans compete while carrying palm tree trunks and passing a baton for several kilometers. Around puberty, boys are initiated into the tribe through a number of rituals, including an ear-piercing ceremony, where wood sticks are put through the earlobes and increased in size as the years pass for the rest of their lives. This ceremony is directly related to one of their creation stories that ended with two trees growing where blood was shed. The sticks are believed to protect them from bad dreams and vicious animals. Girls are trained by village elders in traditional medicine and childbirth rituals. Today, modern technology is beginning to threaten the Xavante way of life due to environmental decay, among other things, but for the most part, the Xavante have managed to maintain their distinct culture through the help of indigenous rights and environmental activists.

YUPIK (YOO' • PICK)

The Yupik live in southwestern Alaska and Siberia. Their own term for themselves is Yuit, which means the real people. Their igloo homes are constructed of packed snow and used during the winter to facilitate seal hunting through holes in the ice. The rest of the year they live in A-shaped wooden houses. Traditionally there were men's houses (qasqig) and women's houses (ena) right next to each other. Boys lived with their mothers until about age five, at which time they would move in with the men. The Yupik etch decorations on ivory harpoon heads, needle cases, and other tools, and carve sculpture on ivory, walrus teeth, or soapstone. They are well known for their traditions of leather-work, singing, and storytelling. The passage to manhood for a Yupik boy occurs when he kills his first seal and shares the kill with every member of the community. At this point, he has developed the essential attributes of being a man—knowledge and respect for the animals. The Yupik believe in a supreme rule of all sea animals; annual ceremonies of thanksgiving are performed in honor of the souls of seals and whales.

ZULU (ZOO' • LOO)

The Zulu, made up of numerous tribes, each under an independent chief, live in the Natal province in the Republic of South Africa. During the nineteenth century the Zulu leader Shaka united the tribes to create the powerful Zulu nation. Zulu economy was based on cattle and grain farming, but today Zulus work mostly in South African cities and mines or on farms. Traditional Zulu religion was centered on ancestor worship, on belief in a creator god, and on rainmaking rites performed by the ruler. One of the most important religious events for the Zulu is the Feast of the First Fruits. Today Christianity coexists with traditional Zulu beliefs; traditional healers, or isangomas, are important and often work within the healthcare system. Zulus now live in urban and rural areas and are involved in national politics after their severe oppression during the apartheid.

NOTE FROM THE AUTHORS

We started this project hoping to share with our own children the world
and its peoples in all their wonderful diversity and knowledge. Sadly, many of these
tribes are in danger, because of environmental and economic pressures, because
of globalization and its assimilative tendencies, because of insufficient laws
and protection. In the doing of the book, we consulted anthropologists and activists,
who have generously read and vetted the information contained here. If we have
inadvertently erred, or worse, offended, please accept our sincere regrets.

The book is an offering, a celebration and a reminder, that respect for all peoples
is something that needs to be taught to be learned.

Tribal Alphabet
By Claudia Pearson and Nan Richardson
An Umbrage Editions Book

Tribal Alphabet copyright © 2008 Umbrage Editions
Illustrations copyright © 2008 Claudia Pearson
Text copyright © 2008 Nan Richardson

First Edition ISBN 978-1-884167-71-3

An Umbrage Editions book
Publisher: Nan Richardson
Exhibitions Director: Temple Smith Richardson
Editorial Assistant: Ashley Singley
Copy Editor: Oriana Leckert
Designer: Unha Kim
Consulting anthropologist: Veronica Davidov

Umbrage Editions
111 Front Street, Suite 208
Brooklyn, New York 11201
www.umbragebooks.com

Distributed by Consortium in the United States and Canada
www.consortium.com

Printed in China

Special Thanks to Ellen Lutz, Director of Cultural Survival, for her support.
To know more about how to help indigenous people, please contact them at:
Cultural Survival
215 Prospect Street, Cambridge, MA, 02139
www.culturalsurvival.org

RENFREW BRANCH

A Australia
B Spain
C North America
D Mali
E Russia
F Fiji
G Belize
H Thailand
I Philippines
J Andaman Isles
K Turkey
L Mexico
M New Zealand

N Colombia
O Ethiopia
P Borneo
Q Peru
R Bulgaria
S Finland
T Sahara
U Uzbekistan
V Romania
W Senegal
X Brazil
Y Alaska
Z South Africa